2 Bed Room –

1 Bedroom lofts –

Ashland – 3

450 + utilities

1 of each.

4 hrs/ week

JIMR@ASU.edu

THE STUDENT REVOLUTION:
A Global Confrontation

YMCA

480 - 965 - 5555

Tim Russell

statement

– Secondary –

– Insight –
nights.

1 semerster

Sept 1st dellive

apply online

lept test score
Query form
Resume
recomendations
transcripts

Coe admissions@
ASU. edu

THE STUDENT REVOLUTION:

A Global Confrontation

BY JOSEPH A. CALIFANO, Jr.

The Norton Library

W · W · NORTON & COMPANY · INC · New York

SBN 393 00519 4

Library of Congress Catalog Card No. 77-95881

Published simultaneously in Canada by
George J. McLeod Limited, Toronto

PRINTED IN THE UNITED STATES OF AMERICA

3 4 5 6 7 8 9 0

To   *Trudy, Class of 1954*
        Mark, Class of 1984
        Joseph, III, Class of 1985

Contents

Author's Note

This book grows out of a deep concern about the relationship between the young, particularly the college students, and the adult establishment. Step by step the war between these groups is escalating as clearly as the war in Vietnam escalated in 1965 and 1966.

There was no chance to look at this subject in any depth during my time in the Pentagon and at the White House. However, two days after President Lyndon B. Johnson left office, I departed, under a Ford Foundation grant, on a trip to ten countries to look at the question of youth and the establishment abroad. The countries were in Europe, Africa, the Middle East and Asia.

I visited London, Paris, Bonn, Berlin, and Rome. In the Middle East I visited Israel; in Africa, Kenya and Tanzania; in Asia, India and Japan. (I declined to go to Latin America, not because the students were quiet there, but because many other writers had examined the problems of Latin American students.) A significant portion of this book is a result of that trip.

The profound commonality of factors affecting students abroad so intrigued me that I decided to spend a good deal of time at home reading about the subject and talking to others more expert than I. Finally, I was encouraged to "put it all together" in a book. This book represents that effort.

The reasons for writing it are simple. Few, if any, other Americans have traveled around the world looking at the student problem. Too few Americans, Europeans, and Japanese recognize the profound crises of values and beliefs through which their younger generations now suffer. Even fewer recognize that the determination of the young to do something about it is not merely an Ivy League fad.

Particularly in the United States, youth has been in the vanguard of many of the recent cutting issues. It was the college students who went south to sit in at lunch counters, ride on buses, and march to Selma with Martin Luther King. It was the college students who first began to put up the stop signs on the Vietnam War. They are the ones who turned Senator Eugene McCarthy—albeit briefly—from an enigmatic dreamer to a Presidential candidate. It is they who are pressing for the most significant reform in the structure of the Democratic Party in its history.

Many of the students feel that they are "corrupted" and "co-opted" by society. But my hunch is that it is the students who "co-opted" Doctor Spock and Gene McCarthy and that what they are trying to do now can, for the next several years, place them in the vanguard of the attack on some of our basic social problems.

There are too many people to thank to even try to list them here. Let me mention only McGeorge Bundy, the brilliant president of the Ford Foundation; my tireless secretaries, Evelyn Furgerson and Ann Bailard; and my wife and children who suffered through the many drafts and to whom this book is dedicated.

THE STUDENT REVOLUTION:
A Global Confrontation

Introduction

"The students are like nymphomaniacs; no amount of university reform will gratify their appetites."

"The present youthful agitation . . . contains, in the minds of better students, ferments and demands that can become useful and fruitful if they find greater trust and understanding on the part of adults."

"Problems at the universities are no different from the problems that parents have with adolescent children. University administrators are no more willing to deal with them than confused parents, and when they do, they exercise just about as much maturity as adolescent students."

"The students are undergoing a crisis of belief. For years professors have taught them to be skeptical of every moral doctrine, religious belief and political philosophy. Today we are reaping the harvest of those seeds."

"Berkeley showed the students of the world they could grind a university to a halt. Columbia drove the point home, and that is just what we intend to do across Europe."

"This is nothing more than a passing fad, turned global by the phenomenal advance in mass communications media."

"The students really want to destroy all the structure of society; they will not be satisfied with destruction of the university system alone."

"The authorities are afraid to discipline, much less shoot or hit the students because they are the sons of the bourgeoisie."

"The students want to stop the train. It is moving too fast, and they are afraid they will become numerical eunuchs, castrated and filed on IBM cards in the technological post-industrial society."

"The students are suffering from a breakdown in family structure and an anything-goes sexual freedom."

These were some of the typical comments made by university presidents, Pope Paul VI, distinguished journalists, professors, members of Parliament, mayors, government officials, and students and youth leaders in a variety of countries I visited in Europe, the Middle East, Africa and Asia early in 1969. There is at least some element of truth in all of them. But if anything is clear after such a survey, it is that no one really knows what the root causes of student unrest are.

While there are obvious differences among the problems of the young people in these countries, there are so many similarities, particularly among the developed nations, that it seemed to me worth setting them down. The trip was essentially an impressionistic one, but the impressions were strong, and the experience abroad highlights some important lessons for the United States. The parallels are clear and similarities too often frightening, but the dangers are avoidable—if we act wisely and in time.

Chapter I

The Post-Industrial Countries: Europe

GREAT BRITAIN

I was in London just before the London School of Economics (LSE) was closed down by large numbers of students protesting the erection of gates between the various college courtyards there.

The trouble at LSE had begun two years before, when a student wrote a letter to the London *Times* on school stationery. The letter criticized several practices at LSE. Invoking one of the technical rules of the school (prohibiting the student use of school stationery for such purposes), the LSE administration suspended the student who wrote the letter. (That student, incidentally, was later elected president of the LSE student body.) Almost overnight, a relatively small group of radical students, estimated by school authorities at no more than a hundred out of three thousand, had an issue which gave them an almost unanimous base of support. There was trouble, including violence and some damage at the school, but the police handled it with unusual restraint and prudence, and matters appeared to quiet down.

Two years later, as student agitation rose beyond sporadic incidents once again, LSE Director Dr. Walter Adams decided, as a precautionary measure, to erect gates separating the different courtyards at the school. Immediately, the gates became a physical symbol not merely for radical agitation but for broad student discontent with a variety of practices—a symbol easy to identify and easy to destroy. Shortly after the gates were erected, the students announced they would tear them down, and they did.

Destruction of the gates was not considered a serious problem in London. The police there had decided to accept some measure of physical damage in the hope of avoiding the personal confrontation students were seeking "to bring the violence of British society out into the open." Police officials had quite candidly admitted this to British press officials, on an informal basis, in an apparently successful attempt to gain their understanding during a prior student demonstration.

The symbolic gates brought all of the complaints which had been festering at LSE once again to the surface, and the school was forced to close down. What were those complaints? On the surface, they were so familiar that they seemed like those of students at some American university: inadequate student participation in the decision-making process; not enough contact with professors; overcrowding; courses out of touch with modern-day reality; too many examinations.

Sounding like some American critics of our universities, Maurice Foley, Parliamentary Undersecretary of the British Foreign Office, who formerly handled youth affairs for the Labor Party, told me that most of these and other student

18

complaints about the British university system were well justified, particularly the one about overcrowding and its impact on the British university system. Sitting in his well-appointed Whitehall office, Foley pointed out that the pressure from the student-population explosion had created so severe a need for assistant professors that the British universities were filled with "inexperienced lecturers whose intellectual capability and judgment did not compare with that of British faculties a generation ago."

Another high official in the Labor government said he believed Foley had a valid point, but, that British students suffer from a deep sense that they have no place in the political structure of the nation. "They have set as their ultimate objective not merely the reform of LSE, but the destruction of the Wilson government and representative democracy in Great Britain." Trevor Fiske, head of the National Student Union in England, put it differently: "The students are asking basically one question, 'How does an individual stay an individual in a technological society?'"

Several professors believe that the initial causes of discontent stemmed from the writings of Herbert Marcuse, Mao Tsetung, and Che Guevara, coupled with a general sense of disillusionment about Vietnam, especially the Wilson government's support for United States policy. While these elements—the radical "philosophers" and Vietnam—were present everywhere I visited, in London there was also the issue of South Africa and Rhodesia. More than one bearded English student decried his nation's "racist policies" with respect to those countries: "a disgusting hangover from our colonialist mentality."

The radical students in England, as in other countries, are splintered across the spectrum of radical doctrine. They act as one, however, once an issue worthy of a demonstration arises. And they are beginning to act as one in their attempt to take over the National Student Union.

The National Union of Students is an organization with substantial financial support and a potential for influence far beyond that of any student organization in the United States. Every British university student must pay dues to the National Union of Students while in college. The way in which those dues are spent is largely within the discretion of the Student Union officers and executive board members.

Until recent years, the Union of Students has been a sort of U.S.O. for British students. Its concentration had been on providing welfare services and financing social functions. More recently, however, as the radical students have recognized the enormous financial resources available through control of the Union, the organization has become much more politically oriented. Trevor Fiske, its president during 1969, confessed to me that the Union had waited too long to get into the political arena and, as a result, left an unnecessary vacuum for radical organizations. He also indicated that the stakes are so high for control of the National Union of Students that fights were becoming more and more vicious and intense during election campaigns and at executive board meetings. Nevertheless, early in 1969 the Union was still in control of moderate liberals. The issue, of course, is whether the National British Student Union will lose control to the radicals and become the British version of the Japanese Zengakuren (Student Union). For rebellious students are determined to "politicize" and "radicalize" the organization.

FRANCE

The Sorbonne and Nanterre—and, indeed, in Paris, I was told, the entire university structure—still suffer from the ravages of what are euphemistically called "the events of May 1968." Complaints are much more vigorously expressed by the French students, and—according to professors at the Sorbonne and Nanterre—university operations appear to be much more severely hampered in France than elsewhere in Western Europe. For example, it has become common practice, both at Sorbonne and Nanterre, for students to make it impossible for some professors to teach their courses or to give examinations.

University conditions, which were involved to a great extent in the 1968 student riots, have not appreciably changed. Courses are still overcrowded. At the Sorbonne, students are not encouraged to attend classes. Several professors and students told me that if all the students enrolled in a course attended classes, they would never be able to fit into the classroom. One professor said that almost one thousand students were taking the course he taught in a room that seated about two hundred students. Many Americans disparage the fifty-thousand-student multi-universities of some of our states, but in Paris there are 160 thousand students under the jurisdiction of the Rector of the Sorbonne alone.

At Nanterre, many comparisons are made to Columbia. The most obvious one involves the location of Nanterre in the center of what is essentially a French ghetto suburb, with no amusements or diversions immediately adjacent to the university for students and with many professors living and working miles away in Parisian suburbs inaccessible to their pupils.

There are substantially more women involved with the radical French students than anywhere else I visited. Although radical leaders were deadly earnest in their desire to bring down the de Gaulle government, in part thanks to the girls, there is a certain French lightheartedness about the student disturbances. Dating during demonstrations is common. There are signs painted on the walls of the Sorbonne reading, "To make love helps to make better revolution."

At least two professors told me they had moved their courses to early morning hours—8:00 A.M. and 9:00 A.M. When I asked why, they responded, "French revolutionaries never get up early in the morning, and there is no disruption of early morning classes."

Paris was the first place in which I encountered two elements clearly apparent in Japanese universities and beginning to come to the surface in our own country: 1) more than one professor originally sympathetic to the radical students had moved to a position of opposition, because he thought the radicals would destroy the entire university community; and 2) although no young professors would admit it, two of the older professors at the Sorbonne told me that their young colleagues were intimidated by the radical students and that this was affecting their academic objectivity. Similar charges were made by older professors at the University of Bonn and the Free University at Berlin.

As was the case in London, Berlin, and Bonn, the center of radical sentiment in the French university appears to be in the sociology departments, which in American terms would cover not only the traditional sociology courses, but political science and many of the humanities.

Sociology faculties and students are not the only instigators of unrest, although they rapidly work their way to the forefront. Where university conditions are particularly appalling in other departments, as in the medical schools of the universities of Rome and Tokyo, students at those schools have initiated the demonstrations. I was told by one Italian journalist that until the 1967 demonstrations at Rome University, a medical student graduated without ever having worked on a cadaver. In Tokyo, the life of an intern is characterized as "near slavery," even by some professors at the medical school.

The immediate objectives of the radical students in France has gone beyond their early cries for university reform comparable to those requested by students at the London School of Economics. Once they tasted the near-demise of the de Gaulle government in what a recent book calls "The Almost Revolution" of May 1968, the French students set their sights on joining the workers again and bringing down de Gaulle. They claim a great deal of the credit for de Gaulle's fall after the defeat of the May 1969 referendum.

The rebel students consider representative democracy a failure. Radical students in France and elsewhere argue for some kind of Utopia where everybody votes on everything that affects them. Students in France are almost universal in their verbal condemnation of the French university, the Vietnam war, and the corruption of capitalist society.

One should not get the impression, however, that the radical students are of only one mind. In France, there are nihilists following Nietzsche; Maoists following the Red Guards; Castroites urging permanent revolution; Trotskyites wanting revolution without Stalinism; and just plain, old-fashioned anarchists and free-loving hedonists—both somewhat more active than their predecessors. And, as one professor said, "within each of these groups, there are splinters." But the radicals are capable of acting in concert during demonstrations, if not before or after them.

The French experience provides perhaps the most dramatic example of the strong anti-Soviet communist trend among the radical students abroad and their difficulty in working with labor unions. For a brief period during the May 1968 events in Paris, the communist-led unions and the students joined in the demonstrations that almost brought the de Gaulle government down. But they very soon parted ways.

Why? Because of the students' bitter attacks on the Soviet-style communist labor leaders and French communist party, and the fear by the communist labor leaders that their union members were becoming so antagonistic to student antics that they would no longer follow them. In Germany, numerous student attempts to form a coalition with the workers have failed. In Italy, striking workers have thrown students off their picket lines and out of their parades when students tried to join them in fighting for union demands.

This raises another interesting facet of the student radical philosophy. Wherever I went, both student and academic radicals cited the French experience (and the increasing establishmentarianism and conservatism of the working class in their country) as convincing evidence that the revolution must come first from the student-university community. "We constitute the revolutionary class today; we are the only uncorrupted adults in a corrupt society," was the way one British student put it to me.

I do not want to give the impression that the anti-Soviet feeling of the students in France or anywhere else is as sharp as their anti-Americanism. It is not. Among all hard-core radical students and among the vast majority of left wing and liberal students, anti-Americanism is one of the foremost common characteristics. But to rebel students abroad, Soviet society is not the panacea it was to communists in the 1930s. The Czechoslovak invasion is considered as bad and immoral as the Vietnam war, which radical French students consider to be a totally unjustified and immoral act by the United States and the nadir of international political morality today. The underlying theme, however, is "a plague on both your houses."

WEST GERMANY AND WEST BERLIN

Bonn appeared to be a relatively quiet university town, at least by current standards. There, university officials have moved quickly to meet some student demands (although only after the students broke into a faculty meeting and disrupted it). Requests for increased student power in the areas of university administration, selection of faculty, and course structure were apparently being met in a prudent and progressive way. The director of the university, while denying students the right to vote at faculty meetings, was permitting them to observe all but executive faculty sessions. However, requests for elimination of all examinations and objective standards were rejected out of hand. Significantly, there were more than one professor like Hans-Adolph Jacobsen, who was working directly with the radical students. Communication has not been permitted to break down.

The Free University in West Berlin presents a peculiar situation, and it is easy to see why it has been the chronic center of radical German student activity. Students attending the Free University are exempt from the West German draft. This draft exemption tends to attract a disproportionate number of pacifists and radical students. In addition, a significant influence may be the element of release from the oppression of East Germany among the students recently escaped through East Berlin. While the center of activity in Germany appeared to be switching to Frankfurt early in 1969, as a result of the shooting of students during a riot there, the Free University is likely to continue to be a student hot spot.

The radical German students, coincidentally called the SDS (*Sozialistischer Deutsche Studentenbund*), are estimated to represent less than one percent of the German university student body (fewer than two thousand of 260 thousand). Nevertheless, they are generally acknowledged as the European experts in student riot methods and tactics. They claim to have learned a great deal from radical Japanese students, and it is generally believed, by British academics and government officials, that German SDS students have assisted their English colleagues on more than one occasion.

While university officials throughout Europe told me their government officials were afraid of the political dynamite buried in the student issue and hence were abrogating their responsibility to act, nowhere was this more strongly expressed than in West Germany. There the issues—particularly as university administrators see them—are political, not academic. Even the university-oriented student protests involve matters largely for government, rather than university action: issues like modern facilities and higher university budgets.

The intensity of this feeling came sharply to me when a recently-resigned director of a German university castigated, in my presence, members of the three major political parties in Germany—the Christian Democrats, the Social Democrats, and the Free Democrats. The politicians had turned the student issue over to professors, he said, because it was too hot. But the professors had no power to deal with it. He charged Parliament members with failing to provide resources for the greatly expanded university population and failure to get their political organizations interested in students. He said they had abandoned the entire student arena to the radicals and the communists. This same charge was made just as strongly by at least one professor in Japan who told me that the Liberal Democratic Party had done "nothing, absolutely nothing to organize students along more traditional, moderate lines."

To my surprise, the three members of the German Parliament pleaded guilty, although they injected a partial defense. They claimed that the students were not interested in the moderate political parties and that all attempts to interest them had failed. They did admit, however, that the attempts had been too gingerly made. They also agreed that the coalitions among the German political parties had contributed substantially, if not primarily, to the student view that there were no longer any alternatives among the political parties in Germany. The Christian Democrats and Free Democrats form the governing coalition in West Berlin; the Christian Democrats and Social Democrats form the governing coalition in West Germany.

A top Bonn University Administrator makes essentially the same point in a somewhat different manner: "If all faculty meetings are to be open to students and there are to be no executive sessions permitted, then the next step is to open all Parliamentary Committee meetings with no executive sessions permitted. We are fighting the battle for the politicians and the government of Germany, and they are not giving us the support we need."

In Germany, as later in Japan, professors and political figures raised the question of athletics for the students. The German establishmentarians believe that the current generation of students needs more athletic activity as an outlet for their energy. They think the current German establishment's revulsion against athletics (resulting from overemphasis during the Hitler regime) has contributed to the student search for other outlets.

German professors are by no means without blame. Several told me that it is common practice for some professors to have their written notes read by a student to his fellow students rather than lecture in person. Moreover, even when unnecessary, professors change their notes from year to year to increase sales. Students must have these notes to pass examinations, because classes are frequently so overcrowded that attendance is discouraged.

ITALY

It is the Italian students who have characterized the student revolution as a total or global confrontation. They see it as global in two aspects: geographically and ideologically, a world-wide attack on the moral values of modern society and on the corrupt and non-responsive institutions of the Establishment.

While all radical students condemn Soviet communism and American democracy, most are more vehement in their attack on the American system. Radical Italian students (occupying a large portion of Rome University while I was there) are more evenhanded (if not fair) than any others in expressing their opposition to both representative democracy and Soviet communism. For example, above the entrance to the law school at the University of Rome hung a sign which said: "Down with

Russian and American imperialism." Italian students condemn with equal vigor Vietnam and Czechoslovakia, American economic investment in Western Europe and Russian economic domination of Eastern Europe, the North Atlantic Treaty Organization and the Warsaw Pact.

In Italy, students were for the first time turning their attention to the NATO Pact. While university and government officials considered this to be of virtually no importance in terms of Italian politics, it was interesting to note NATO as an issue there. For in England and France many journalists and university and political leaders predicted that as the Vietnam war subsided and the Nuclear Non-proliferation Treaty became a ratified document, NATO would be the next major issue that the radical students would mark for protest and eventual destruction.

As in the case of other Western European countries, the immediate university-oriented concerns of the students involved more contact with professors, overcrowding, irrelevant courses, and more student power in university matters. The professor-student contact problem appeared to be more serious in Italy than in any other country visited.

Typically, Italian university professors live in Rome—whether they teach in Naples, Venice, Milan, or elsewhere. If they teach outside the city, they customarily go to the university for perhaps one day (sometimes two) a week. A professor living in Rome and teaching in Venice would be comparable in our country to a professor living in Washington, D. C., and teaching in Boston!

Furthermore, it is not uncommon, particularly at the University of Rome, for professors to have full-time jobs outside the university. Many members of the Italian Parliament are also full professors at the University of Rome. Many full-time practicing lawyers are full professors at the University of Rome. I was told that even a few corporate executives have maintained their full professorships at Italian universities.

The impact is devastating on both the students and the younger faculty members. Students rarely, if ever, see their professors personally in the classroom, much less individually. One distinguished Italian journalist told me he had graduated from the University of Rome without ever attending class after the first year: "The professors were never there: why should the students go?" Since the number of full professorships is virtually frozen, young assistant professors are bitter about slots to which they aspire being held by professors who have no intention of pursuing the academic life.

In Italy, there are noticeable rumbles among the high school students. At dinner one evening at the home of one of Italy's most distinguished intellectuals and writers, Luigi Barzini, one of his sons, a 17-year-old, amazed me with his knowledge of the Italian anarchists, perceptions of hypocrisies in Western and Soviet society, and mastery of Marxist theory. He was a high school senior and all for the "global confrontation" urged by Italian university radicals.

Italian university administrators do not share the rage of their German counterparts about the lack of backbone of their political leaders. Nevertheless, resentment at the ambivalent nature of government support was apparent at the University of Rome. For example, fully half of the time I spent with the Rector of Rome University involved a discussion of the reluctance of Italian government authorities to provide the necessary police support and political backing to deal with hardcore radical students.

Chapter **II**

The Post-Industrial Countries:
Japan

Compared to their European counterparts, the Japanese radical students seem to be relatively well organized and financed. They are doggedly earnest about bringing down the Sato government. Almost any issues, and particularly those with some anti-American flavor, can bring out thousands of students in Tokyo, Kyoto, and other cities with large university populations. As the *Economist* has pointed out, "The Zengakuren demonstrations are not spontaneous; from the organized columns to the wooden staves, iron bars and empty milk bottles provided as ammunition, everything is minutely planned."

Japan was the only nation I visited with any noticeable student right wing, which I found only among the athletes. It is quite small and not nearly so vocal as the hardcore radicals. A vociferous minority of students were activists—radical or Mao-communist—and in either case noisy and articulate. A larger number were "moderate" (which in European terms is usually to the left of the liberal Democrats in America) and for the most part apathetic.

The university-oriented targets of the Japanese radical students are similar to those of their European colleagues: over-crowding, lack of contact with professors, meaningless courses, inadequate student participation in the decision-making process.

There are factors unique to the Japanese student: his family life before entering the university and the too-often shocking living conditions at the university. Usually a male Japanese who is headed for college spends all his years—preschool, elementary and secondary school—working much harder than his European or American counterpart to prepare for university entrance exams. Going to the university is an extraordinary high point of his life. Once he arrives there, usually from a very protected and intimate home life, he discovers that the mirage of a fountain of knowledge is in reality a pretty scrubby cactus. Nowhere is this brought home more clearly than in his living conditions at or near one of the big-city Japanese universities. They are close to (and in some cases below) the poverty line. The result is, of course, a psychological and physical revulsion and frustration hard for an American to comprehend and easy for any radical to exploit.

Japanese Communist Party students (JCP's) have assumed the moderate role. They shrewdly oppose violence by students and, publicly at least, assert that university and social reform should be worked out through institutional processes. The radical element in Japan—called the anti-JCP's, the anti-communists—seems to be more destructive than in any other country I visited. Some portions of Kyoto University, after the riots in late February and early March, 1969 looked almost as though they had been bombed by hand grenades. There were buildings in which virtually no doors remained on hinges and every window had been shattered.

The police in Japan may be the most sophisticated in the world at handling student riots. Police officers in Japan are subjected to intensive training and rigid discipline standards much more comparable to U. S. Army Military Police than local police force training in our country. The results show not in terms of protecting property but in moderating the extreme potential of violence against human beings.

Despite this enormous destruction in Kyoto and elsewhere and their remarkable restraint, the Japanese police are still on the defensive. This apparently stems from deeply-rooted anti-police sentiment that has carried over from the regime preceding and during World War II. Moreover, Japanese police officials are quick to charge that TV news commentators and most show business personalities are sympathetic to the students and against the police.

The top security people I met talked candidly and with little apparent bitterness. They admitted to their problems and said that, as a result, they had taken steps to put down student riots with an absolute minimum of direct contact between the police and the students. First, they eliminated, to the greatest extent possible, weapons immediately available to students during a riot. Among other things, all cobblestones around universities have been paved over. (This was also done around the Sorbonne after the riots in May 1968.) U. S. Embassy personnel told me that, ingeniously, the Japanese police have devised enormous bumpers, which they attach to trucks, capable of extending from one side of the street to the other. They drive these trucks, behind shields, slowly into the students to force them back. In addition, the Japanese police frequently use huge nets which they drop on students.

With all the student trouble in Japan, it is believed that only one death has resulted, and this death, according to the police, involved radical students getting control of a police car and running over a Japanese rioter. The gun control laws are so strict in Japan that students are either unable or afraid, because of the severe penalties, to possess firearms. I was told that a sentence of several years for illegal possession of a firearm is not uncommon for a first offender in Japan. As the students become more violent (Molotov cocktails are now becoming part of the Japanese student arsenal), the number of injuries and perhaps deaths is likely to increase.

More clearly than in any other nation, student unrest is on the rise in Japan, and there appears to be no university reform that will allay it. It is directed openly, ultimately and violently at the Sato government. Even its immediate political targets are relatively long-range for student rebels: the reversion of Okinawa to the Japanese (presently under discussion between United States and Japanese representatives); the United States-Japanese Security Pact, which comes up for renewal in 1970; and a determination to disrupt and hopefully destroy the World's Fair to be held in Osaka next year. The radical students' hope is to replace the pro-Western Sato government with at least a neutral regime—and some students would say with a pro-Chinese, anti-U.S., anti-Soviet regime.

Japan was the only country where officials flatly stated that Communist China was helping the radical left with funds. * They also felt that the moderation of the Communist Party student group in Japan in part reflected the Russian-Chinese split.

Japan was the only country where government officials made their statistics available to me, and they are worth reporting, for they illustrate that three can indeed make a revo-

* In West Berlin, it is generally believed that the East Germans provide steel helmets and torches to demonstrating students, but no one in an official capacity would unequivocally confirm this to me.

lution. There are 845 "universities" in Japan, 377 of which provide a full four-year course. The rest are essentially two-year junior colleges. 1.27 million of the university students attend the four-year course (although they have eight years in which to complete it); * the remaining 230 thousand university students go to junior college.

Of this enormous student body, only about eight thousand are members of the radical/anarchist left; twelve thousand are Communist Party members. The eight thousand radicals are, in turn, split into numerous groups. Yet this small percentage of communists and radicals—less than 1.5 percent of the students—effectively control 519—more than 60 percent—of the 845 campus Zengakuren organizations, and of course, the National Zengakuren. Dues-paying membership is compulsory for every student in Japanese universities (they pay four years' dues upon entrance as freshmen), and the Zengakuren controls the use of those funds.

To appreciate what this means in American terms, one would have to assume that: 1) more than sixty percent of the student councils on every college campus in the U.S. was controlled by a numerical minority of radicals or communists; 2) every student going to college had to pay four years' dues to his college student council as part of his entrance fee; 3) each college student council in turn had to pay part of those dues to the National Student Council (controlled by communist and bitterly factionalized radical students); 4) both at the national and the campus level, the student councils were free to spend the money virtually as they wished: for anarchist propaganda, helmets, clubs, to harass professors and university administrators, to recruit high school students, etc.

In Japan, government officials state that this is precisely the way a large part of that money is spent.

Japan was the only country I visited where students quite

* In most Western European countries, there is no time within which a university student must complete his work.

openly intimidate their professors and university presidents. While I was there, several professors and administrators at Tokyo and Kyoto universities were being held prisoner by the students who were subjecting them to self-criticism sessions in an attempt to obtain confessions of guilt of crimes against society. Once again, to translate into American terms: imagine Roger Heyns, or John Kenneth Galbraith or Father Hesburgh locked in a room, put through a self-criticism session and ultimately forced to sign a confession of crimes against society as the price of his freedom! *

In terms of successful disruption of university (and, in some cases, even national) activity, the Japanese radical students appear to be, by far, the most successful in the world. Tokyo University was paralyzed by a student strike throughout 1968. It took eight thousand policemen two days to evict radical students from the main hall of the University in January 1969—a two-day siege, similar to the later one at Kyoto, which ended an occupation that had lasted for over six months.

Even at that point, the troubles of Tokyo University were not to abate. For in late February and early March 1969, radical Japanese students successfully prevented the new freshman class from taking its entrance examinations. It thus appeared that there would be no freshman class at Tokyo University for the subsequent school year. What were the freshmen to do? The radical students had a ready answer: devote a year of their lives to the reversion of Okinawa, the elimination of American bases in Japan, and the disruption of the 1970 World's Fair in Osaka.

* I should point out that the Japanese police moved into both universities while I was in Japan. In a pitched battle (lasting over two days at Kyoto), they freed the professors and university officials.

Chapter **III**

The Pre-Industrial Countries

The Japanese and Western European scale of student unrest is nowhere approached in India, Kenya, Tanzania, and Israel. (Israel is included as "pre-industrial," though the description is less appropriate to that country). All those countries are in a state of development where trained young people are desperately needed and immediately employed (with a notable exception for engineers in India) in the public or private sector, but always where their country needs talent and almost always in a way in which they feel they are contributing to making their nation better. Israel is perhaps the most outstanding example. The Israeli students I met were consumed with a desire to help build their nation.

There is a special aspect to the Israeli student, however,

which should be noted. All male citizens of Israel go into military for three years at age eighteen. Thus, the typical Israeli college freshman is about the same age as is the typical American college graduate. Moreover, in addition to the maturity of years and military service, almost all Israeli students have been touched personally by war during their lives. Surrounded by national enemies, they are much closer than their European colleagues to the reality of survival in a very explosive situation.

Even there, however, the university is not without student problems both university-oriented and on a national scale. When I talked to three student leaders and several faculty members at Hebrew University, it became immediately clear that there are two festering issues there. At the university level, the issue involves the relationship between government and religion, somewhat comparable to church-state issues in the U.S. It arose in the winter of 1969 on the question whether the university swimming pool should be open on the Sabbath. Orthodox Jews wanted it closed for everyone; the other students (by far the majority) wanted it open. With no tradition of separation of church and state, the Orthodox Jews believe that it is wrong for *anyone* to use the pool on Saturday. The resolution? After a student referendum, the decision was made to keep the pool open, but to close the parking lot near it so students will have to walk several blocks to get there. An incident was avoided in this case, but the real issue is much broader.

The students at Hebrew University also complain about the aging nature of the Israeli Parliament. They point out that Israel has the oldest ruling clan in the world with the possible exception of Red China: the average age in Parliament is well over sixty. They argue that the time has come to replace the pre–State-of-Israel leaders with a new generation unencumbered with the "hangups" (their word) over the fight to create a State of Israel.

Israel was the only country I visited which had a youth-student problem even remotely approaching our black student problem. The difference between the Oriental and European Jews is analogous to the difference between black and white Americans. And the European Jewish students—as well as several professors at Hebrew University—are mounting a serious and substantial campaign to better the lot of their Oriental colleagues. The effort involves improving the educational level of the Oriental Jews; it has eschewed lowering scholastic standards as a distinctly counterproductive course of action.

In Kenya, Tanzania, and India, the element of survival amidst enemy countries and the requirement of universal military training upon graduation from secondary school is not present. Nevertheless, with rare exception, there is an element of economic survival and patriotism not present in the affluent West European, Japanese, and American societies.

One cannot sandwich between visits to Western European countries and Japan discussions with students and the young in Israel, Kenya, Tanzania, and India without being struck by the sharpest difference of all: there is virtually no sense of nationalism in the post-industrial countries, while there is a pervasive and intense spirit of nationalism in the pre-industrial countries. The relatively affluent, sophisticated Western European students abhor nationalistic instincts. While the young Japanese lack the active anti-nationalistic spirit of the young West Europeans, no Japanese student with whom I talked discussed, with any enthusiasm, Japan as a nation. Even the reversion of Okinawa is seen among many Japanese students more as an issue of opposition to American imperialism than an issue of nationalism. The sense of fatherland is dying fast in the post-industrial countries, and there are no young mourners. The radicals are waiting to dance on the grave; the moderates will not even attend the funeral.

Quite to the contrary, nationalism runs deep in the less-developed countries, particularly among the youth. Kenyan youth, with a purer sense of capitalism than we now have in America, are deeply committed to the future of their nation. In Tanzania the young—in this case, socialists—talk about nothing else. In both of these African countries, when the young travel abroad, whether to the United States, Europe, or the Soviet Union, they seek to learn skills they can bring back to their homelands to build their own countries. The vast majority of Indian youth—even the most supercilious and arrogant among them—are essentially directed toward the future of their own country. They are proud of it, and they want to solve its problems.

The implications of this sharp difference between the pre- and post-industrial countries are difficult to perceive. But the first step in clear perception is a recognition that nationalism is dead among youth in Western Europe and dying in Japan. It is very much alive in Israel, Kenya, Tanzania and India.

Chapter **IV**

The Common Elements of Student
Unrest in the Post-Industrial Countries

Anyone who has talked to any number of students knows how fiercely individualistic they try to be and often are. If the students had any set of ten commandments, the first would be: "Be yourself; be an individual; be separate from the rest of society." This is apparent by merely looking at students: their dress, their mannerisms, even their haircuts.

It is with some trepidation, therefore, that I attempt to set forth the common elements of student unrest in the post-industrial nations I visited. I do so because of a firm conviction that there are some specific, profound, and generally-misunderstood threads that run through virtually all radical student movements abroad. Identifying those threads is of enormous help in understanding the young there—and in our own country. For the similarities are striking.

Here are the common elements I found in the post-industrial countries:

1. *Invariably, the number of hard-core radical students is quite small.*

I was able to obtain "hard" figures only from Japanese government officials. But in no country did anyone, even the radical students, believe they constituted more than four or five percent of the student population. British Student Union President Trevor Fiske estimated the hard-core radicals and communists combined at three percent. In most countries, the radicals were estimated at one percent of the university population, and then only at some universities.

Yet invariably, the institutions and numbers that radical students control or can mobilize are sufficient to create serious problems. In at least two areas I visited—Japan and West Berlin—members of Parliament told me privately that students, if not handled carefully, were capable of bringing down the government.

2. *The objectives of the radical students are extraordinarily fuzzy, but they are directed at the whole fabric of modern society, not merely at the university. In many cases, students admitted to having no immediate objective at all, except destruction.*

The typical radical student argument I heard scores of times ran along the following lines:

"We are not sure what kind of society we want. We know that we do not like the representative democratic societies we live in, and we do not like Soviet Communism, with its inhuman control over

41

the individual. Both are dehumanizing, and equally so.

"We do not know what kind of society we would replace them with, but they must be destroyed. To find out what kind of society will come out of this destruction, we must go through the experience of the revolution. Perhaps we will discover that we must remain in a constant state of revolution."

This last point is usually made when the listener cites the aftermaths of most violent revolutions in terms of stringent control over individual freedom, mass executions, and the like. As Jacques Bosquet, the Deputy Director of the UNESCO Division of Education, has pointed out:

Students are, therefore, challenging the whole fabric of present-day society; they do not limit their demands to a few minor reforms, but call for a radical transformation.

They share, with considerable theoretical or practical variants, a number of common ideas: distaste for the cheap glitter of a commercial society, which leads to alienation in the sociological and psychiatric senses of the word, questioning of a university education which aims at turning students into the future leaders of this alienated society, desire to give free rein to their imagination and instincts in spite of all "repressions," refusal to separate work and leisure, and rejection of consumer culture.

Or, again, as the radical students put it: "Representative democracy and Soviet Communism are inherently violent societies, super-sophisticated in disguising their violence to the individual. All we are doing is bringing that violence into the open."

German professors who lived through the Hitler Youth

Movement put it in another, considerably more frightening way. They see the radical students as near-Fascist anarchists, reminiscent of the young Nazis who beat up professors deviating from the Hitler line in the 1930s.

One corollary of the breadth of the student objectives is that university reform is unlikely to satisfy the radical hard core, or even significantly hinder their ability to broaden their base. Until recently, when the action switched to Frankfurt, the most serious problem for Germans was at the Free University at Berlin—a university where students attend faculty meetings, vote on the Board of Trustees, and even have two votes on the group that selects new professors. All this, before the recent trouble! As one of the leading professors in Germany told me, "The greatest myth of us liberals is that university reform will ease student discontent."

3. *Radical students verbally reflect significant influence by romantic notions of Mao, Castro, Guevara, Marcuse, and—in Italy—some of the old anarchists; but the students are in a very real sense undergoing a crisis of belief.*

They invariably speak a Marxist jargon, but if any philosophy guides them, it is an acutely aggressive anarchism. This anarchism bears little relationship to the eighteenth-century anarchists, who pursued their cause in a nonviolent, almost academic manner.

In Italy, for example, at the annual convention of the Italian anarchists, several students (including, I was told, Daniel Cohn-Bendit) attended the first sessions. Shortly after the sessions began, they attacked the old-line anarchists bitterly and at first tried to disrupt the meeting. Within a relatively short time, apparently out of boredom as much as anything else, they left the meeting, many of the young revolutionaries going off to the southern coast of Italy for the deeper pleasures of Italian women and wine.

The quotations of Chairman Mao, Guevara's diary, and the

works of Marcuse, while cited by student radicals across the
world as a modern-day Koran, are more probably tools, expe-
dient and currently popular, than an enduring philosophical
base. The rather sharp difference reported to me of the treat-
ment of Marcuse in West Berlin in 1967 (wildly applauded by
fifteen hundred students) and 1968 (shouted down by German radical students) and the demonstration against him by
Rome University students in June 1969 give some support to
this proposition. In Japan, the radical students have a fetish
against heroes of any kind (including Mao); at negotiating
meetings with faculty members, for example, a different student leads that side of the table at each meeting to avoid any
"hero cult of the personality."

Beneath all the jargon, however, I sensed a profound crisis
of belief on the part of the vast majority of all students—a crisis that provides the nerve for the radical students to touch.
Students simply do not know what to believe. Everywhere
they look in the society around them—the church, the university, the world of business and politics—they see hypocrisy.
And a significant number of students see hypocrisy more
clearly in their own families than anywhere else. Throughout
Western Europe, affluent students talk bitterly and angrily
about parents who are nominally Christian ("they go to
church on Sunday"), but who spend all but one hour a week
consumed in a search for greater material satisfaction. They
claim they are condemned and reprimanded for their own exercise of sexual freedom by parents "to whom adultery has become a way of life because they failed to use the freedom they
had when they were young."

The almost total skepticism of modern Western universities
has had a significant impact on the students. Many professors
(particularly in France) told me that they were concerned
about the way they had consistently poked holes in almost
every political, religious, and moral theory of Western Civilization. They felt this was compounded by their failure to pro-

vide students with any philosophy of life or politics beyond a sort of hedonistic and materialistic liberalism, to replace the gods whose feet of clay they had smashed.

As a professor in the Divinity School at Kyoto said to me: "eighty percent of the students in Japan have no religion whatsoever; about twelve percent are Buddhist or Shinto; the rest Christian." One professor in France noted that one of the major strengths of the radical students was that they were convinced they had *the only morally right* theory of life and society at this time, and that they satisfied in sensitive students the need for some kind of guiding principle.

This righteous attitude accounts in large measure for the major divergence between student radical rhetoric and action. While the hard-core radical students repeatedly cite the need for every man to speak out and vote on every issue that affects him, at this point in time, this appears to be the last thing they want. At the London School of Economics, for example, Colin Crouch, a recent student leader of the liberal left, pointed out that the radical hard core specializes in non-democratic tactics to take control of student organizations. Once they get control, Crouch continues, they hold meetings on minimum notice at inconvenient times, to make certain they cannot be outvoted. In Germany, the radical students oppose secret ballots.

Throughout Western Europe and Japan, there is a strong feeling on the part of the radical students that they should have a special place, at least initially, in setting the standards and determining the future courses of action for their colleagues. This may be relatively simple to achieve. For with all the ferment at the Free University in Berlin, in December 1968, when student elections were held, only forty-one percent of the students voted, even though they had four days in which to cast their votes.

One of the most dramatic examples of this philosophy in action is the disruption of meetings at which speakers anathema to the radical hard core appear. When radical students are questioned about this, they respond that the right to free speech is relative, that all ideas are not worthy of expression or attention, and that they have a positive duty to prevent the spread of anti-revolutionary diatribes. In London, for example, radical students feel fully justified in taking any step necessary to prevent Enoch Powell, the right-wing English segregationist, from speaking on any college campus in the country. At the University of Essex, radical students are proud that their demonstrations made it impossible for a government scientist to lecture on germ warfare in May 1968. There is a tendency here remarkably similar to the eighteenth-century puritanism of the New England Calvinists.

4. *Affluence is unquestionably a significant factor in student unrest.*

Students for the most part do not have to concern themselves with their future in terms of their ability to eat, live in a decent place, clothe themselves, and have a fair share of luxuries. As professor after professor across Western Europe put it: "This generation of students does not have to work to eat." With no need to be concerned about the essential material things of life, they are free to turn their energies to other concerns.

Numerous professors and students told me the students were concerned about the "psychological brutality" of modern society. There is more than a little truth when students speak of the emotional and mental strain created by pressures for conformity, by the environmental horrors of congestion and pollution, and by the convergence of a variety of repressive social pressures as they see themselves growing older.

Even more professors, however, said that students were spoiled: they had too much money from home and too much free time at the university. That upper-middle-class students are at the forefront of the rebels is too frequently the case to be merely a coincidence. And, as often as not, the vanguard radical students are in their fifth, sixth, and, in some cases, eighth year at a university where their work should have been completed in four years.

5. *In asserting the need for more individual freedom from the complexities of technological urban life, the young have struck an immensely appealing chord across post-industrial societies around the world.*

There are few adults or teenagers in the United States, Western Europe, or Japan, who are not irritated by the bureaucracies in which they work and play, or by the government bureaucrats with whom they must deal with increasing frequency as cities become more crowded and life more interdependent. The annoyance with authority is everywhere present as it intrudes more and more into our personal lives. Its occasional arbitrary exercise affects more and more of us personally each day.

The crisis of authority is not limited to universities; it can be found in the church, in government, in unions, to say nothing of the home. As Pope Paul VI has stated, the student rebellion is "a reflection of the crisis of authority which is besetting the modern world." The Pope, with his quiet dignity and white robes, spoke far more profoundly and sympathetically than anyone else about this problem and the emotional and spiritual turmoil through which so many students are suffering. I felt as I sat listening to him that he recognizes the extent to which students are youthful reflections of so many problems of the modern adult world's crisis of authority and belief.

The psychological impact of this crisis on those in authority trying to deal with student unrest can be near-paralyzing. And the students know it. Even if they did not have the intuition to sense it (which they do), they can read it every day in the newspaper and hear it every day in the conversations of their

47

parents and teachers. Is it any wonder that the young will no longer accept authority for its own sake but insist that those who wish to exercise it prove that each attempted exercise is right and necessary?

6. *University conditions are often abominable in Western Europe and Japan.*

The explosion of the student population has staggered university systems around the world. Today, for example, roughly twenty percent of all Japanese between the ages of eighteen and twenty-two are in universities. Prior to the end of World War II, only twenty percent of Japanese teenagers went to high school. The numbers tell the story around the world:

UNIVERSITY STUDENT POPULATION

	1950	Year Indicated
Germany	116,360	260,000 (1968)
France	139,593	600,000 (1968)
Japan	384,795	1,500,000 (1968)
Italy	148,170	593,144 (1966)
England	85,421	184,799 (1966)

Overcrowding has reached almost unbelievable proportions in many of the large universities abroad, and far more than physical facilities have been strained. There are just too many people at universities who should not be there. They either do not need a university education for what they intend to do, or they are incapable of absorbing a university education on the level at which it should be taught. One professor at Bonn University estimated that at least twenty percent, and probably more, of the students at German universities were not mentally equipped to be there and should be in some sort of technical schools. In France, I was told that twenty-five percent of the Sorbonne students were not qualified to be there.

As professors tend to teach toward the middle of their class, the brighter students are unchallenged, even though the inadequate students remain unable to absorb what they are being taught.

Moreover, to meet the demands of increasing numbers of students, many professors told me that the academic standards for young teachers had been decreasing over the past decade in their country. A high official of the Wilson government, also a Labor Party expert on youth affairs, said, "The quality of assistant professors has vastly diminished over the last ten years. Today, too many are not fully qualified and are too young for positions of such responsibility." The result is a combustible mixture of frustrated students and too many incompetent young professors, both pressed into an obsolete university environment in which they do not belong.

While the student violence abroad has gone too far, too many professors have left themselves wide open for legitimate student criticism. Even the most distinguished teachers in Western Europe spend too much time and energy writing books, consulting governments and corporations, in seminars away from the university with their colleagues, and, as one German professor put it, "plotting to go to Harvard or Yale." Teaching students has been the least demanding, time-consuming, and interesting of their various duties, and the students have just become fed up. For even when these professors have appeared in the classroom, too often they have evinced little interest in whether the students understood what they were teaching.

In defense to this charge, some professors and university administrators are quick to point out that the students are spoiled and that parents are asking the university to provide a level of care and feeding they refused to give their own children. There is some truth in this claim. Parent after parent to whom I talked abroad is asking the university to do for his child what he himself has failed or neglected to do. One can

argue that the university has done a remarkable job since
World War II to "straighten out" (typical parental terminol-
ogy) so many students (children) for so long. But this is no
defense of what is going on in many universities abroad.
David Astor of the London *Observer* sums up the point this
way: The university officials find it just as hard to act in an
adult manner with their students as parents do with their teenage children. They are either too strict or too permissive. They
pursue their own interests, which too infrequently coincide
with those of their students. They refuse to listen to legitimate
complaints for so long that the students take illegitimate action to attract their attention.

7. *The traditional left, center, and right parties have failed
grievously in two respects: they have abandoned the student
as an object of political interest, and they have refused to give
the universities the resources and support needed to meet the
demands of the student-population explosion.*

Years ago, the major political parties of Western Europe
were very much in evidence on university campuses. Recently,
however, the traditional parties have either not tried to sell
their political philosophy on the campuses of the world, or
they have tried gingerly and failed miserably. The field has
thus been left wide open for the radical anarchists, communists, and other extremists.

As one French student put it, "The politicians don't give a
damn about anything except their own careers. By the time we
shook them up and reminded them that we were around, they
had ignored us for so long we no longer cared that they failed
us. After all, if they were sincere, we wouldn't have had to riot
in the streets to get their attention."

Is it any wonder that the vast majority of moderate students
abroad agree with the analysis of their radical colleagues that

what began as pragmatic, humanistic liberalism in the first half of the twentieth century has become a selfish and hypocritical libertinism in the fifties and sixties?

Equally important, the governing parties have neglected to provide anything near the resources necessary to ease overcrowding, modernize school facilities, fund and create technical schools, and attract and train able teachers. The universities need money and lots of it. The governing parties have so far shown little inclination to provide it—the taxpayer revolt does not stop at our shores; it is as global as the student revolution.

8. *The immediate situations that precipitate riots are remarkably similar.*

First, take a small group of hard-core radical students constantly probing for an issue to broaden their base of support.

Second, take instant communications at least within the immediate geographic area of the incident.

Third, toss in a mistake by the established authorities.

By and large, most students agree with Trevor Fiske: "The quickest way to broaden the base of the radical students is by unfair discipline." At the London School of Economics, the crucial mistake was the disciplinary action against the student who wrote to a newspaper criticizing the university; at Frankfurt, the shooting of students; at Paris, police brutality. In the United States, when the Students for a Democratic Society demonstrated against the Peace Corps at Oberlin, they had little student support. But, as Thomas Brooks pointed out, when the demonstrators were disciplined outside the normal channels, student opinion rose to their defense and Oberlin was disrupted for a while.

For a first-class donnybrook capable of doing serious and lasting damage to the university involved, it may be essential (and it certainly helps) to have several faculty members on the side of the radical hard core. This can be of critical importance if the objective is to immobilize the university.

In many cases, particularly in non-communist countries, the cards in this area seem stacked against established authority. As long as radical students can probe and probe, again and again, without serious reprimand, anyone in authority is almost bound to make a mistake at some point, particularly when that "authority" is split or has insufficient sanctions for enforcement.

The students unquestionably chose the university as their battleground because it was most familiar to them. But even if they did not recognize its weaknesses at the time they chose the target, students quickly realized that for purposes of direct confrontation, they had selected perhaps the weakest link in the establishment's structure. As Raymond Aron, the brilliant, deeply distressed French professor and writer, told me, "The students have discovered that professors are paper tigers who depend upon the gentlemanly kindness of students for discipline and order. And the radical students are neither gentlemen nor kind to professors."

Particularly in a physical confrontation, faculty meetings with their interminable theoretical debates are no match for an aggressively led, single-purpose group of radical students. Moreover, until recently, the professors were furthest removed from "the real world," as one distinguished London editor told me. Virtually every professor with whom I talked decried the cumbersome administrative procedure that inhibited firm action by university authorities and admitted that they, and most of their colleagues, lived in an "unrealistic ivory tower." A French professor put it as well as anyone: "Universities with their split faculties, inexperienced in political negotiations, with no force to back up their position, are the weakest institutions in the Western World."

9. *I found no evidence of an international conspiracy among students (except for occasional assertions that the Chinese Communists were putting funds into radical student movements). The similarity in student tactics around the world is striking, but it is largely attributable to the enormous impact of the media, particularly television, and the increase in student travel.*

When American students at Brandeis University took control of the telephone system there, within ten days British, French, German, and Italian students attempted to do the same thing at universities in their own countries. When asked about it, many of them said they saw the Brandeis incident on television or read it in a newspaper. Students watch each other's techniques to see what succeeds and fails.

Berkeley is the example most often cited by the European radical students, although they applaud the near-radicalization of Columbia in 1968. The British are particularly sensitive about Berkeley and the American civil rights movement. Almost invariably, they tended to blame a great deal of student unrest on the American example at Berkeley and the wide support in America for the tactic of the civil rights movement to break unconstitutional laws in order to test them in court. As evidence, British professors and journalists cited the presence of former Berkeley students like Marshall Bloom, among the hard-core radical leadership at LSE and Oxford. I suspect, however, that there is considerable validity to the remark of the student leader who said, "We got as much from the British ban-the-bomb demonstrations as we did from the American civil rights disorders."

While the French professors attribute some of their trouble to American students attending the Sorbonne, and to the example of Berkeley, they do not repeatedly cite this as a major cause. The Germans, on the other hand, tend to put more em-

53

phasis on the Japanese and French students as the horrible examples contributing to German student unrest. Even the German professors, however, point out that a few Berkeley students were part of the radical hard core in German student riots last year. If any student group can be identified as exporting anarchy in recent years, it would have to be the Americans.

Thus, while there is no conspiracy as far as I could tell, two enormously powerful elements are at work: mass media, particularly television; and student travel. Many European professors feel so strongly about the explosive influence of American students that they are examining with meticulous care their applications to come to their universities. This is particularly true in Britain, where a few Berkeley radicals have been consistently and publicly identified among the leaders of British student demonstrations.

There is an important distinction between the nationally run university system of Western Europe and Japan and the independence of individual colleges in the United States. As one professor said, "Here in France what happens at one university immediately affects all the others, because they are all part of the same system. In the States, what happens at Berkeley or Columbia does not immediately touch Princeton or Yale because they are independent institutions."

10. *The students in Western Europe and Japan are distinguishable from the students behind the Iron Curtain and those in what I have called "pre-industrial nations" like Israel, Kenya and Tanzania.*

As a Czechoslovakian student said to his colleagues from London, Paris, and West Berlin while we were in London, "We have a clearly defined objective—we want liberty. We do not know what you want but we do know you are abusing the liberty you have." One Israeli student told me: "We have no time for such nonsense. We have a nation to build and a war to fight." His colleagues nodded agreement. Young Kenyans and Tanzanians, who have studied in the U.S. and Western Europe, simply cannot understand what all the shouting on the university campuses is about.

11. *While there has been remarkably little visible backlash, it does exist, and the politicians are watching it carefully.*

The most frequently cited backlash example in Europe and Japan is the resounding support for de Gaulle after the student-worker riots in May 1968. Yet, in 1969, de Gaulle fell, and the students take a great deal of the credit for his demise. While I was repeatedly told that middle-class workers were increasingly impatient about students' antics, the only specific evidence of action I found in this area was in Birmingham, England, where the local authorities withdrew support from the university after student disturbances; and in Italy, where workers threw students out of their strike parades.

The issue is extremely volatile, however, and politicians are watching with care. For example, if the situation in Japan continues to deteriorate, more than one member of Parliament told me, Sato would be wise to run against the students. He felt Sato would win an overwhelming victory, unobtainable if he had to run on his pro-United States policies. In West Germany, there was some fear of a turn to the right as a result of the student disturbances, but no German with whom I spoke was deeply concerned about it. In Italy, there was so much upper-middle-class sympathy with student demands for university reforms that a backlash among Italians with direct experience at the major universities seemed unlikely in the immediate future.

There was everywhere, however, a distinct uneasiness about which way public reaction to student rebels would turn. Legislation was pending or being prepared for the parliaments of

West Germany, West Berlin, and Italy. There was a variety of bills under discussion in all those countries roughly comparable to the spectrum of legislation proposed and discussed to handle the student and university problems in the United States. Most members of parliaments were carefully preserving their options as they studied this problem and their own future. In doing so, they were reacting with considerably more restraint and understanding than many of their U.S. counterparts and the Japanese Liberal Party, which rammed through anti-student legislation that drew condemnation not only from Japanese students, but from most other political parties in Japan.

Chapter V

Relevance to America

In looking to the experience of student uprisings abroad to see what relevance it holds for the United States, it is important first to note four major distinctions.

1. *There were no black-white racial tensions at the universities I visited abroad.*

Neither the European countries, nor Japan, nor even India with its caste system, has the kind of history of racial injustice that we have in the United States. There has not been festering in those countries the tensions between blacks and whites which have plagued our country from the beginning. Nor is civil rights for minority groups the kind of major emotional and political issue that it has been in the United States throughout the 1960s. Thus the enormously complicating factor of black-white racial tensions is not an element of student unrest abroad.

Most countries, like Italy, West Germany, and Japan, do not have this problem, simply because there is no significant racial minority among the student population. Even in France, with a significant minority of black African students, no racial tensions have erupted. The French experience may not be comparable, however, because for the most part, black students from Africa are not French citizens and have no aspirations to become (either separated or integrated) a part of the French community. As a result, they have no motivation to agitate for a place in the French social and political arena. Black Africans come to France to learn skills to bring back to help improve their home countries.

Israel, as I have noted, does have a problem somewhat comparable to that of the blacks in the United States. This concerns the Oriental Jews, who come largely from the Arab countries and whose educational, health, and social level is sharply below that of the European Jews. However, Israeli political leaders as well as Israeli professors and students, who are largely from European backgrounds, are united in programs to assist the Oriental Jews and to bring them an educational level comparable to that of the European Jews. Though the going is tough, the programs appear to be working.

Of all the countries I visited, England is closest to the United States in terms of racial tension. On the campus, however, there is, so far, no notable black militancy or white racism. Not one student, professor, political leader, or journalist mentioned the subject when I interviewed him. As a matter of fact, a few Negro radicals are among the vanguard of the essentially White radical movement of the London School of Economics which includes David Adelstein, a White South African.

The extraordinarily explosive and complicating nature of the black-white situation on the American campus and among American youth should not be underestimated. The implications go beyond the fact that the black issue itself provides another fuse for student disorders not present on the campuses abroad. That element—the blacks as the spark plug of student disorder—in itself has created a significant amount of trouble in 1968 and 1969.

Much more significant is the fact that during the sixties the young have invariably been in the vanguard on this issue. It was the young white college students who joined the Negro civil rights activists in the South in the early sixties in the host of sit-ins, marches and demonstrations that resulted in the passage of such extensive civil rights legislation. It was the young white students who joined in the early phases of the black power movement, many arguing first for integration of the black movement and then for understanding for separation of the races. It was the young at the City College of New York and Cornell who engaged in what can almost be characterized as "race wars" on those campuses. At Columbia, blacks and whites worked separately, but toward common objectives such as more student control over university policy. It is among the college students that racially-mixed dating is noticeably on the increase.

The point is that the young, particularly the white college students, are at a crossroads in terms of race relations. The white militants join black demands for special black studies programs, for separate dormitories, for the admission of a larger number of black students. At the same time, it is the young college students who, on some campuses, are fighting blacks and black demands. And it is the young blacks who are standing alone, in places like Cornell, not wanting any white assistance as they press for their demands.

The racial issue is all the more complicated because of the confusion among the middle-class white college students about which way to turn on the race question. Suffering from mixed feelings of guilt, shaken values, and an increasing sense of futility about the effectiveness of civil rights legislation and government action in this area; mixed emotions about violence; and a combination of acceptance and rejection from their black colleagues, these students now appear to be at a crossroads, and a difficult one. If the history of the earlier part of this decade is any indication, the way the students turn as they go through this crossroads may be the way many Americans will turn in a few years.

2. *There is no drug problem at the universities abroad and no significant hippie element.*

There is, of course, the mod dress, the long hair and the dungarees and fatigue jackets that have become a large part of the American college scene. However, virtually without exception, the only hippies I noticed in the Western European countries visited were American student expatriates. While I questioned almost everyone about dope, the answer was always the same: That is an American problem, not a European one. Even in India, the students taking dope were American visitors, some of whom had come for that purpose, to see the Taj Mahal and to find a guru.

The presence of the drug problem, particularly in terms of marijuana, adds another complicating element to the student situation in the United States. For, as students see it, marijuana is less habit-forming and less damaging to the health than cigarettes. When faced with arguments about the impact of marijuana on their rationality, those students who use it argue that marijuana is no more debilitating than alcohol. The marijuana problem spills over into one of their more basic concerns about the hypocrisy of industrial society. As Senator George McGovern once put it, "Our society makes millionaires of cigarette manufacturers for peddling cancer; it makes criminals out of young students who smoke marijuana."

3. *The Vietnam problem is ubiquitous and a source of profound distress here and abroad. But abroad the Vietnam war issue is not aggravated by a draft problem which in the United States so alienates students and contributes significantly to the reluctance of university administrators to expel violent students.*

Most countries abroad have either no draft or no war to fight. Israel, which has both, is involved in a fight for survival, fully supported by the entire population of the country. Moreover, the draft there is virtually universal and considered fair by most of the young Israelis.

The inequity of the draft system in the United States has been allowed to fester so long that the issue has become the existence of the draft itself. Virtually no responsible citizen who has looked at the draft has approved of it in its present form. Students are even able to cite Lyndon B. Johnson and Richard M. Nixon as authorities for the proposition that the present draft system is grossly unfair. They have watched for years while Congress has refused to pass the legislation necessary to make it more equitable.

Over those years, the students here have come to believe with increasingly deep conviction—which many are willing to back with action—that the war in Vietnam which they are being drafted to wage is totally immoral and utterly unjustified. Increasing numbers of university administrators and professors, as well as parents, have come to agree with them.

As much as anything else, I believe it is this draft law, particularly in the face of a shooting Vietnam war, that makes university officials reluctant to expel violent students. Expulsion means delivery to General Hershey and likely shipment to

Vietnam. University officials may disagree with their students about the tactics of violence on the campus, but they regard as cruel and unusual punishment the sentencing of students to a dilemma where they must either be drafted to fight in a war they consider immoral, or, if they refuse to serve, subjected to criminal penalties that will scar them for life and further alienate them from society.

The failure of so many high government officials to recognize this in any of the statements they have made about student unrest is a clear signal to the young and college faculties that they simply do not understand what is happening on the campus today. So long as this situation exists, all the talk about backbone and all the threats about enforcing laws and cutting off funds will not move most university officials to expel large numbers of violent radical students. And students themselves—even the most radical ones—are conscious of the need to stay in school. As James Kunen, the bushy-haired student rebel author of *The Strawberry Statement,* bluntly put it, "You can't drop out of school because you'd be drafted. . . ."

4. *There is no marked tendency among the adults abroad— whether politicians or parents—to look upon their student unrest as part of some international (or even national) conspiracy.*

Radical students both here and abroad are firm believers that the establishment is in some kind of conspiracy against the individual. They see it everywhere: in the military-industrial complex, in the defense research contracts of universities and professors, in the correspondence files they rifle, in the idea of the power-élite popularized by C. Wright Mills, in the lack of ideologically dominated and divergent political parties. In this sense, on the student side of the equation the situations here and abroad are generally comparable.

The divergence on the adult side of the equation is sharp.

Whereas it is difficult to discuss the student rebels in America at some suburban cocktail party without becoming involved in a discussion of conspiracy or communism, the subject virtually never arises abroad. When I raised it, the listener was quick to dismiss it. Of course, several professors and government officials believed communists were exploiting the situation. But they promptly recognized that there was a situation to exploit.

Even in countries like Japan, where police officials believe they have solid proof of the use of Red Chinese funds by student radicals, and in cities like West Berlin, where it is strongly suspected that East Germany is providing assistance to rebels at the Free University, there is no strong sense of conspiracy. No one says, "There must be some conspiracy, probaby foreign-inspired, or our young would not be acting this way. Someone is provoking it; we certainly are not; therefore it must be a foreign influence or extremist professors."

The difference in attitude has an enormous impact on the way in which student unrest is approached as a problem by those with power to affect it. While we have become increasingly more sophisticated in our ability to recognize that there may be profound causes for this unrest, not many Americans have said, "Whether there is a foreign influence or foreign funds involved in the student unrest is irrelevant. Unless there was a deeper nerve to touch or a profound distress on which to play, alien funds or influence would have little impact." Such thoughts are commonly expressed in Europe and Japan. I have rarely heard adults voice them in the United States.

These four differences—the absence of black-white racial tensions, the absence of the drug problem, the fact that the Vietnam issue is not aggravated by an inequitable draft, and the lack of any marked suspicions of conspiracy on behalf of adults abroad—must be kept in mind in any examination of the relevance of student unrest abroad to such unrest in the

United States. The similarities, however, significantly overshadow the differences.

Most of the common elements of student unrest in the post-industrial countries are present in the United States. The number of hard-core radical students is quite small. (The best estimates I have seen placed the total membership of the Students for a Democratic Society in 1969 at five thousand to seventy-five hundred, with an ability to rouse about seventy-thousand sympathetic colleagues.)

The objectives of the students in both cases are fuzzy but directed to the whole fabric of society in which they live. While radical students here tend to speak less of Mao, Castro, Che Guevara and Marcuse, they are influenced by a similarly romantic concept of those men and splintered into ideological factions. Affluence is probably more of a factor in the United States than it is in Western Europe and Japan, but it is present in all three places. Severe university overcrowding is sporadically present or just beginning in the United States; in Western Europe it is an omnipresent fact. While the interest of the political parties of Western Europe in students is inadequate, it is greater than it is here. Both here and in the post-industrial countries abroad, the students are touching in their own way on many issues that have broad appeal throughout adult society.

Most significantly, students here, in Western Europe, and in Japan suffer from a profound crisis of belief and have little respect for and virtually no sense of nationalism. As *Fortune* magazine noted in its June 1969 poll, "A majority of college students no longer hold religion or patriotism to be very important."

These similarities, plus the longer history of student unrest abroad—and indeed the differences themselves—highlight, for the United States, some of the most important aspects of our own student revolution.

1. *We must recognize that the young of our country are experiencing a profound crisis of belief—a crisis which many adults share and for which they are, in many ways, responsible.*

For years our students have been subjected, in school and at home, to a relentless skepticism which has not always been healthy. While the skepticism has been unyielding, it has failed to recognize a great deal of the truth in the old Basuto proverb: "If a man does away with his traditional way of living and throws away his good customs, he had better first make certain that he has something of value to replace them."

As I talked with French professors who were concerned about the way in which they had destroyed, as "myths," the political, moral, and religious doctrines of Western civilization, I could not help thinking of numerous American professors who were doing the same thing.

The crisis of belief affecting the student goes far beyond university reform and far beyond radical students. Anyone who believes that university reform will resolve the problems of today's rebellious youth is living in a fool's paradise. Here, as abroad, the crisis of belief goes beyond questions about the relevancy of university courses and the legitimacy of individual professors to teach and higher educational institutions to exist in their present form. It goes even beyond the legitimacy of existing political and social institutions. It cuts deeply across the spectrum of public and private life.

The students are experiencing a crisis which is profoundly religious, intellectual, and emotional, and in my judgment, it goes to the very purpose of life for large numbers of our young people. This crisis of belief is leading to a confrontation as geographically and ideologically global as the wildest Italian radical ever dreamed. It is, more than any other factor, the key to radicalizing, over a period of time, large segments of moderate students.

This profound crisis of belief among our young people has led them to question virtually every value our society once considered essential to its survival and prosperity. As James Kunen succinctly put it: "My friends and I became preoccupied with the common nostalgic assertion that 'these are the best years of our lives.' We could accept the fact that college years are exhausting, confusing, boring, troubled, frustrating, and meaningless. . . . But that everything subsequent would be worse was a concept difficult to grasp and, once grasped, impossible to accept."

The students must be shown that some of their questions can be answered, and that where they can't, change, unquestionably more difficult to achieve than they realize, is not only possible, but much more likely and enduring by peaceful means than by violence.

They desperately look for answers. A few of them find bizarre answers in a search for a philosophy of life. While their parents and teachers may scorn some of these far-out "life styles," there is little derision among their colleagues on the campus. In a revealing article in the *New York Times Magazine*, Father Andrew M. Greeley discussed the "new-time religion on campus"—the increasing interest of American students in witchcraft, astrology, sorcery, Zen, horoscopes, I Chingism, Teilhard de Chardin's omega point. Though those interested are admittedly still a small minority, Father Greeley was surprised that the majority of the students were not only not laughing at them, they actually respected them. The key, of course, lies in the comments of one of his University of Chicago students:

"They really believe that what they say is true. They really believe that they do have the answer and that they know what is ethically right and ethically wrong. It's hard to avoid being affected by their enthusiasm after you've been in a school that really isn't sure what is true or what is right or wrong."

The Students for a Democratic Society—the radicals who

render harsh, but subjectively sure judgments on everything from the university to the world to God—have struck the very same chord. At least, say so many moderate students, the SDS people feel they know what is morally right and they are sincerely acting according to what their conscience dictates as the only morally right course.

The disorder our students see in the philosophies of the adults closest to them—their teachers and their parents—is more profoundly disturbing to them than physical violence which they see in the streets and to which many of them are willing to resort. As Richard Poirier put it in the *Atlantic Monthly*, "More terrifying than the disorder in the streets is the disorder in our heads; the rebellion of youth, far from being a cause of disorder, is rather a reaction, a rebellion against the disorder we call order, against our failure to make sense of the way we live now and have lived since 1945."

I am not propounding any theory of collective guilt or even collective responsibility. Such theories are psychologically unacceptable to me; and in practice they provide facile shields for avoidance of individual responsibility. Moreover, students here, like their colleagues abroad, are quite capable of and intent upon making individual judgments about individuals. Just as professors are singled out at the Sorbonne for disruption of classes and examinations, so here in America many of our students have singled out specific individuals at universities for attack.

Indeed, a key element of the student problem is their horror at the collective subterfuges adults use to avoid individual judgments and disguise their own hypocrisy. The hypocrisy that students see in their elders is a major cause of their crisis of belief. For even where students are given suggestions about what to believe—or substitutes for the theories that are dismissed—like their European colleagues, they find that their teachers (professors or parents) do not live by their teachings.

They see hypocrisy first at the university and in matters affecting the university. They see it in professors more interested in consulting the government and corporations than in teaching; more interested in writing books and articles than in spending time with individual students; more interested in the esteem with which their colleagues hold them than in respect from their students. The young relate this "hypocrisy" to the legitimacy of the status of their professors. They question, in effect, the right to teach, the authority to teach, in those who are more concerned with other interests.

Like their Japanese and European counterparts, they also see hypocrisy beyond the university. They see it in political leaders who state that cities must be rebuilt or that law and order must be maintained but fail to serve up programs or resources to get the job done. They see it in businessmen and labor leaders who do not live up to policies they publicly urge on others. They see it in their own liberal white parents, who argue for equality for all while they live in white suburbia and oppose tax increases. The students see it, as Senator Edward M. Kennedy saw it in a Washington speech before the New Democratic Coalition, in the discipline to which they are subjected for rifling university files, while Otto Otepka is voted a $36,000 job by the Senate for rifling State Department files.

To be sure, there is a measure of adolescence in any such feeling by teenage college students—a feeling of neglect and emotional rejection by father (mother) figures who are not sufficiently interested in them. So they cry out for attention. But as David Astor, publisher-editor of the *Observer,* pointed out to the administrators of the London School of Economics at a luncheon in the *Observer* Conference Room in England: some feeling of adolescence is at least understandable in an adolescent; it is more difficult to justify in an adult.

This adult adolescence is reflected here, as abroad, in a variety of ways: in the return hypocrisy adults attribute to the young and in the doubts some professors have about their own legitimacy. It is also reflected here—but not abroad—in the too-often outer-directed view so many American parents have of the student revolution.

The adult establishment tends to see at least as much hypocrisy in the young as the young attribute to the establishment. It feels that the rhetorical commitment of the young to eliminate poverty, to bring peace to the world and justice to all Americans is rarely matched with the kind of personal commitment necessary to do the job. It believes that, too often, the limit of the commitment of the young ends with a protest in the streets or occupation of the dean's office. It notes how easily the young can say, "We don't care about careers; we care about ideals," because society is so affluent that the idealistic young will eat and drink well no matter what they do. To this extent there is a great similarity between European and American adults.

Unlike European adults, however, an enormous number of Americans tend to believe that there is some outer-directed element which is getting hold of our young people. Who has not heard the parent of a college student say: "My son never thought that way when he was at home. It must be something the professors are teaching, or something he is reading, or someone he met at college." Europeans, unlike Americans, are much more willing to recognize that the most important outer-directed element of the student revolution is that students do not like what they see, hear, and feel in modern society. The distress the students suffer is distinctly personal, and it comes from within.

The most visible result of this kind of adult adolescence is backlash. We see it reflected in legislative proposals, not unlike those pending in Germany and Italy, and passed in Japan, to outlaw or withdraw funds from students who engage in disruptive activities. We see it on boards of trustees of universities which fail to understand the complex problems with which their college presidents must deal. We see it among college alumni who threaten to withdraw financial support unless "something is done about the radical students."

Finally, adult adolescence is reflected both here and abroad by an increasing tendency among some university professors to question their own legitimacy—their own authority to teach.

Charles Frankel, in his perceptive book *Education and the Barricades,* points out that we are living through a crisis of legitimacy. He sees it as having aspects of the kind of crisis caused when the standards by which an existing regime justifies its existence are challenged by rival standards—a crisis such as Christianity created for the Roman Empire. Frankel also sees it as the kind of crisis which comes when a society fails to legitimize itself in its own terms; when it fails to do what its own rationale calls for it to do.

The crisis of legitimacy of which Frankel writes exists. In many cases there is a justification for questioning the legitimacy of institutions. The problem with so many adult adolescents in our universities and elsewhere among the liberal community is a failure to distinguish between the significance of personal morality and institutional morality in terms of the legitimacy of the authority exercised. John Courtney Murray, the brilliant American Jesuit philosopher, used to point out that one of the key problems of the world was the confusion between the standards of morality which govern individual activity and the standards of morality which govern a nation. The application of institutional moral standards to human beings—or individual moral standards to institutions—creates enormous problems for both.

Put in the present context, a professor of philosophy or religion or family life does not need to be, in his own personal life, a faithful husband in order to teach his course well and in order to teach his course legitimately. To hold otherwise would be to deny that man has a human nature—to deny that

70

he is fallible. Because of his very nature itself, it is easier for a man—a human being—to teach a philosophy of life than to live by it. The failure of an individual teacher to live entirely by a philosophy he propounds does not mean he has no legitimacy as a teacher of that philosophy any more than it means that the philosophy he is teaching is wrong. The failure of those in authority, particularly some academics, to recognize this has led an increasing number of them to question their own legitimacy as professors. Once they do this, they are conceding one of the most philosophically insidious and potentially dangerous hypotheses propounded by adolescent radical students.

Thus, there is a mutual adolescence which leads too often to a mutuality of superficial concern and slogans. Where else does this mutual adolescence lead? Most unfortunately, it is the genesis of an enormous area of mutual suspicion in this country which far exceeds anything I found abroad between the students and the establishment. Under such circumstances, the trust essential for the solution of any difficult problem between the two is simply not present. This trust is the *sine qua non* for any solution of the student problem. Without it, temporary amelioration founded in shrewd tactics may be possible, but nothing more. The first step may be an identification of some basic level of values that the generations (for lack of a better word) share: a recognition, for example, by each that the other, in part at least, is finally seeking honest answers and is entitled to some measure of respect.

2. *The students must be given a greater measure of real control over their own lives and the things which affect their lives—in their words, "a piece of the action."*

Perhaps as well as anyone, Paul Goodman has caught the feeling of many students (as well as many other Americans) with his phrase, "the psychology of being powerless." Many of

71

our students fear that the underlying conditions of modern life may be beyond their power to influence. The technological and population explosions seem inevitable and uncontrollable. Hundreds of thousands of Americans further congest our society as they outrun each other in the race for urbanization. Bureaucracy is everywhere, even in the life of the student: in the disciplinary and grading systems of high schools and the nationwide college-board entrance examinations tests, upon which the student must depend to get into college, only to meet another, similar system upon which he must depend to get into graduate school; only to meet still another, similar system upon which he must depend for fruitful employment. And what does he see upon graduation? More bureaucracy: big unions, giant corporations, cumbersome impersonal government at every level and, inevitably, long, forgettable sets of numbers which identify each of us.

As Goodman pointed out: "Our psychology, in brief, is that history is out of control. It is no longer something that we make but something that happens to us." The sphere of effective power for an individual seems increasingly limited. Inevitably, he insists upon more control over his own life and the things which affect it. No individual feels this more keenly than today's college student.

He feels it just as much abroad as in the United States. The demands of Sorbonne or Rome students mirror those of our own: more control over courses; more control over administration; more control over faculty—more control.

Even where the specific issues differ, the point is the same. In France, where the university system is centralized in the government in Paris, the students want decentralization. In Germany, which has the most decentralized university system in Western Europe, the students want centralization. The immediate objectives of the students appear to be exactly opposite. But one only need talk for a few minutes to a pretty, black-haired radical girl at the Sorbonne or a blond, husky German at Bonn, and he will realize that the real objective is not centralization or decentralization, but more control over the things that affect their lives.

As Kirke Hanson of Stanford University said in *Look* Magazine: "Students are approaching the Establishment, trying to discover if they can have greater control over it. One of the themes on our campus might be termed 'impotent outrage.' We want so badly to have an impact on the society in which we live."

Nowhere is this more apparent than in the intense opposition to the Vietnam war—an opposition that has become an almost singleminded obsession to the vast majority of American college students. This is an issue on which we are not dealing with a limited number of radical students, for anyone who has been on a campus during the past year cannot help but feel the intense student opposition to the war. They had no control over the start of the war, and have little to say about its conduct, and General Hershey doesn't consult with them before they are drafted.

True, there is opposition abroad. But while the demonstrations are noisy and vocal, they lack the intense personal involvement present here. As the students put it, "The only people who have to fight that war, who have to give up a part of their lives for that war, and who might even die in it are the young." The students here see it as a war begun and waged under policies of both political parties, in a manner which has virtually no impact upon the vast majority of adults in our society.

For the establishment, it is business as usual. There is no need to give up anything except to pay a slightly higher price for the goods and services which are still readily available to all and to pay perhaps a little more taxes and delay the purchase of the third car or the larger house. In short, except for those unfortunate Americans whose sons are killed or maimed in Vietnam, only the young suffer the ravages of this war, and the young have the least control over it.

This is not a polemic either to end the war or to put students in charge of our foreign policy. Vietnam was selected here only as the most potent example of the impotence that the young feel over their very lives. The end of the war is likely to temper student unrest significantly, but only temporarily. The end of the war will no more mark the end of student unrest than the death of Moses ended the search of the Jewish people for the Promised Land.

This is, however, an argument to give students more power —and responsibility—at least in some fairly obvious areas of immediate personal concern to them. Let me give a few examples:

There are clear reasons why young Americans are not yet equipped to sit on the National Security Council, but certainly they could be represented on local draft boards.

Even assuming the enactment of a random selection system of the kind proposed by both Presidents Johnson and Nixon, the area of discretion for local draft boards is enormous and is likely to remain so. According to the 1967 Report of the National Advisory Commission on Selective Service, the average age of Selective Service board members is fifty-eight. Twenty percent—one in every five board members—is over seventy; four hundred are over eighty; twelve are between ninety and ninety-nine! Is it too much to ask that our young people be given at least one seat on each local draft board in the country?

I think we would find them surprisingly mature and, in many cases, fairer, indeed stricter than their elders. The Uniform Code of Military Justice gives an enlisted man, at a general court martial, the right to insist that enlisted men sit on the five-member court. Nevertheless, it is almost an axiom of uniformed defense lawyers that enlisted men will be tougher than officers in rendering judgment of guilt or innocence and fixing a sentence. We might just find a roughly comparable situation if students were put on local draft boards.

It may even now be too late for a proposal like this. Students might refuse to serve on local draft boards lest they become the Uncle Toms of the peace movement. The students might see it as "co-opting"—giving in to an attempt by the establishment to lure them away from their revolt by making them part of the "system." But they would not see it as a "fraudulent co-opt," like sitting on powerless advisory commissions of the type we now have. At least, under this proposal, students could have a piece of the action—a vote and some control. Even the more radical students recognize the difference between, as they put it, "a fraudulent and legitimate co-opt."

Students could have a voice at the highest level of Federal government which sets educational policy.

In France, Minister of Education Edgar Faure, after the May 1968 disturbances, placed around him more than one student, like André Safir, whom I met in Paris. Safir's role was roughly that of a special assistant to the top policymaker in the educational community in France. At a Paris restaurant, the energetic young student told how he had traveled extensively around the campuses of France, helped shape and lobby for the educational legislation to give French students a voice in University policy, which was eventually proposed by de Gaulle and passed by the Parliament. The legislation was not all that either Safir or the de Gaulle administration had asked for. But because Safir had lived through the experience of getting it passed, he recognized what an enormous step forward the French student referendum was, and he was wholeheartedlly stumping campuses across France to get students to vote in the referendum. This, less than a year after he had been on the streets of Paris helping lead the rebellious students!

75

Clearly, in this country, the Commissioner of Education, if not the Secretary of Health, Education and Welfare, should have more than one student taking part in his decisions on higher education policy. I am not speaking of a White House Fellows type of program where bright young Americans spend a year in the government to observe and learn. The role I propose would be that of an active aide to the top policy-maker.

Students must be given a greater role in the government of the universities of which they are a part.

So many universities are making changes in this area that it hardly seems necessary to belabor the point. But students increasingly feel the changes miss the point. Whatever the merits of ROTC training on campus, it should not be necessary for students to resort to demonstrations to raise the issue. Whatever one may feel about university expansion into the ghetto neighborhoods, the place for resolution is not on the street.

An essential step—though by no means a solution—in getting these issues above the campus-demonstration level, where hopefully a more productive exchange in an environment of mutual trust can take place, is to give the students a voice at those levels of institutions which lead to decision-making. Predictions are always dangerous in this area, not only because human beings are fallible, but because there are hard-core radical students bent on destruction. Nevertheless, one cannot help believe that if more universities followed the example of Kingman Brewster at Yale there would be less disruption on the campus. For a simple reason, the students at Yale have the feeling that they have a voice in university policy: Brewster has given them a voice. Under these circumstances, the ability of the radical hard core to broaden their base of support is sharply diminished, at least as far as university issues are concerned. Personally, I would not hesitate to give students (or recent graduates) a voice, not only on boards of trustees but even on faculty committees designed to choose other faculty members.

Most easily, students could be placed in charge of student discipline—the control of the personal and social lives of their colleagues vis-à-vis the university. There is no better way to instill the kind of responsibility and mutual respect for persons and the property of others than to charge the students themselves with drawing up the rules necessary to govern their own society and to provide the disciplinary measures and judicial system needed to assure that those rules are enforced fairly. Of course, they will abandon all parietal rules. But my belief is that, rather than *Harrad Experiments* across the nation, we are likely to see little, if any change in the sexual life and personal morality of our college students.

Some residual authority would remain with the university officials who bear ultimate responsibility, particularly in cases of massive disruptions and violence. But there are ample precedents in our national life for such arrangements, the most obvious of which is the relationship between the states and the Federal government with regard to civil disturbances.

The young could be given more control over their government and over the public and private programs designed to channel their energies more constructively.

The eighteen-year-old vote is the most obvious proposal. Giving the eighteen-year-old vote to a young American provides—at least in terms of the one-man-one-vote rule—as much elective political power to the student as his father has. Enactment of the constitutional amendment and laws necessary to grant an eighteen-year-old vote to young Americans should come promptly.

Numerous congressmen and virtually every major potential candidate for the Presidency are firmly on record for this change. President Nixon has joined former President Johnson in recommending that the Congress take action to accomplish this.

As President Johnson said, "The time has come to grant our young what we ask of them but still deny—full and responsi-

77

ble participation in our American democracy. . . . Each time before, when America has extended the vote to citizens whose hour has come, new vitality has been infused into the life-stream of the nation and America has emerged the richer." Whatever else adults may think about the antics of American youth, their hour has come.

Failure to follow this kind of rhetoric through with the action necessary to make it a reality will serve only to create yet another hypocrisy issue for the young radicals. And, although this issue may lack the passion associated with the draft, it certainly provides as broad a potential base of student support.

The Peace Corps, Vista, neighborhood legal services and many community-action programs of private charitable organizations and the Office of Economic Opportunity are excellent examples of imaginative and progressive government policies. But why couldn't recent college graduates be given a chance to run some of these programs? If a twenty-one-year-old can be President of a student body of fifty thousand students, he might just be able to handle a few thousand Vista volunteers. At least, he could be given the opportunity.

Admittedly, there are relatively few high-level positions (like running Vista) available or even appropriate for the recent college graduate. To affect most young Americans with a potential interest in government service, a vast change in Civil Service regulations is essential. A group of young Federal employees has already laid down their initial demands in a pamphlet, *The Condition of the Federal Employee and How to Change It,* published in June 1969. They want a greater opportunity to participate in discussions of policies before they are formulated, even though the decision-making power rests with others. They want jobs judged on the basis of ability rather than seniority. They want more widespread use of the "five-year float" policy, now used in the Peace Corps, limiting professional personnel to five years, to assure a regular personnel turnover and the introduction of new ideas. They want

78

more than is reasonable for the efficient and just operation of the government. But much of what they want is likely to make the government more efficient and just.

3. *It is imperative that the major political parties—the Democrats and Republicans—focus energy and attention on the political interests of students.*

With the rare exception of senators like Robert Kennedy and Eugene McCarthy, both the Democratic and Republican parties in our country have done little to attract and interest the student while he is at college. Their concerns have been with the voting-age public beyond college. As a result, they, like their counterparts abroad, have left a political vacuum of major proportions. While the Communist Party to date has had little success in our country in moving into this vacuum, it is clear that radical-anarchist groups, some armed with romantic views of Mao, Guevara and Marcuse, are having an enormous impact on many of our brightest students. Although I was repeatedly told that the overwhelming majority of the students abroad are fed up with the small radical element, the speaker invariably decried the apathy of his fellow moderates who were permitting so few to destroy their chances to learn.

The eighteen-year-old vote would certainly help increase the interest of the major political parties in youth. Even with the vote, however, it will not be easy for the Democratic and Republican parties to attract the attention and loyalty of large numbers of American students. Student notions judge politics and politicians with an idealistic harshness. The idealism of youth does not appreciate the practical realities of a mayor trying to get more money from a governor or a congressman or a senator making the compromises necessary to make progress in a representative democracy. Students are much more ideologically oriented than either political party. They remain unconvinced of the benefits of having only two major political parties, especially when each is peopled by individuals representing a broad spectrum of ideological views.

Nevertheless, for a variety of reasons, there are elements in both parties—ranging from the intelligence and glamour of a Kennedy, Muskie, or Lindsay to the energetic magnetism of a Harris, Mondale, or Percy—capable of attracting students to the traditional party structure in the country. Because students are generally more liberal than their elders, the heavier burden here falls upon the Democratic party. If the lessons of Western Europe and Japan are any indication, failure of the major political parties to attract vigorous and bright students will only enlarge the vacuum for radicals.

4. *We must face the fact that a four-year university education is not appropriate, necessary, or fulfilling for every American boy and girl. Indeed, in many cases, it can be counterproductive for the individual and destructive for society.*

We must meet head-on the problem we are creating by making a four-year college degree the necessary prerequisite for almost any kind of employment, short of digging a ditch. There are now and will continue to be millions of jobs which require either no college training or some sort of specialized training that could be given in a shorter period of time. It behooves our government and educational institutions to begin dealing with this problem on a large scale. The alternative is a further overcrowding of our major universities and proliferation of second- and third-rate small universities throughout the country. This is perhaps one of the most relevant lessons of West European and Japanese experience. They have increased their university population far beyond their national needs and the needs of their individual citizens for fulfillment. And we appear to be hell-bent on the same course.

I do not underestimate the difficulty of the citizen-education job which must be done to remove the sharp social distinction between vocational school and college, even junior college. But the attempt must be made. For, if the experience abroad is of any value, it shows that the current trend will only keep the campus caldron boiling and spilling over into more and more facets of American society. The reported decision of Rutgers University and the near decision of City College of New York to lower their standards, admit anyone, and enlarge their teaching staffs almost indiscriminately are appalling.

In every West European country visited and in Japan, the lowering of standards, for students as well as for teachers, to accommodate the student-population explosion, caused trouble. Students who did not belong in college were frustrated because they could not make the grade. Brighter students were frustrated because their talents were not challenged. And second-rate professors had insufficient reason to respect "obsolete, anti-revolutionary" concepts of academic excellence.

To the extent there are valid social reasons to increase the number of black, Mexican-American or other minority group students in a university, those students should be given the necessary tutoring and special courses to bring them to the level where they possess the qualifications for admission. Indiscriminate admission of unqualified students is historically a road to educational and societal disaster. To regard the university as society's instrument to make us all productive human beings and socially conscious citizens is to grossly distort its purpose. Such a concept confuses the university with elementary and secondary schools and the home. Those college students who press for this role for our universities are making the same mistake their parents make when they expect four years on a campus to do what eighteen years in the home failed to get done.

There is no reason why business and government (in its role as employer) should not take a look at the thousands of jobs for which they now require a college degree and establish more realistic qualifications related to the job. Where special training is required, business can surely provide it, and probably in a more effective way than universities. To the extent that the humanities broaden a man's horizons and increase his enjoyment of life, an expanded and improved adult education program could go a long way in helping this need.

5. *The governing administrations—Federal, state, and local —must provide the resources necessary to finance the burdens placed on universities, high schools, and elementary schools by the student-population explosion.*

There is no getting around the need for substantial funds for our universities and lower-level schools. Even if additional taxes are required, the investment should be made. Our university population has increased from 2.7 million in 1950 to seven million today, and it is likely to increase further. Our colleges are so much better off than their European and Japanese counterparts that many foreigners wonder what all the shouting is about here. But our universities can get to look like many of those abroad, and they will unless they have the resources they need.

The high schools of urban America are already there. They most nearly resemble the overcrowded, obsolete physical plants of many universities of Europe and Japan. It is the urban high school students who have the most legitimate complaints about poor teachers, courses that are irrelevant to their present situation (much less their future), overcrowding, and the like.

Problems are coming in the high schools of America just as surely as they have come to Japan and are coming to Italy and West Germany. While those Western European students who have studied at or visited American universities find it hard to understand what American college students are complaining about in university-oriented terms, they would see quite familiar conditions at almost any large urban public high school in America.

The Students for a Democratic Society already recognize this. They have begun an attempt to organize the high schools of the country and have produced at least one pamphlet, *High School Reform: Toward a Student Movement*. At Palisades High School in Los Angeles an underground paper has been started. Similar papers have been started at other California high schools. At one, thirty high school students destroyed their student activity cards and "sat in" in protest of a student body assembly being called off for the third time.

In the SDS high school pamphlet, the first set of demands are laid out: creation of a joint student faculty council; the rights of students and teachers to decide collectively upon their courses; no more than twenty-five persons in a class; "an end to student police squads and oppressive attendance officers, replacing them with a voluntary honor system"; and "the right of students to take or not take courses as they see fit." Perhaps the most interesting aspect of the SDS proposal for high school students is the stress they place on getting "our parents active in PTA" and "making a concerted effort to get PTA support"—but they specifically point out that they must not be "co-opted" by their parents, they must lead them.

The demands may seem preposterous to many readers, but there are enormously difficult problems in our urban high schools. The complaints about obsolete physical plants, filth, overcrowding, inadequate facilities (from athletics to laboratories) are legitimate for virtually every public high school in the major cities of this country. The longer they are allowed to fester the less preposterous demands like those in the SDS pamphlet will appear to be.

True educational reform involves not merely the university, but the entire educational system. It will require enormous financial and human resources. With no other reason, this fact alone puts the problem right at the door of our political leaders at every level of government. For the money required must come from them and the people who elect them. The schools cannot possibly raise it.

I realize it is easy to write facile prescriptions for the problems of our students and their relationship to the establishment. I recognize the enormous energy and imagination it will take for the traditional political parties to attract their attention and loyalty. I appreciate the difficulties of the national administration (to say nothing of those of the states and cities) in obtaining adequate funds for our elementary and secondary schools and universities. But I also believe that the stakes here involve not only American youth (and that would be serious enough), but an articulate and increasingly influential segment of our society—a segment, in my judgment, quite capable of influencing those who can tear our democracy to shreds —unless those energies are directed to these problems and funds are spent to eliminate legitimate complaints.

As the mayor of a major European city told me, "The situation has long passed the point where passive reaction will suffice. Some positive and imaginative action is necessary and necessary now!"

At the same time, our students here in America would do well to look at their Czechoslovakian colleagues and remember that it is one thing to fight for freedom where it does not exist and quite another to abuse it where it does.

Chapter **VI**

Quo Vadis

"To say that youth is what's happening is absurd. It's always been happening. Everyone is nineteen, only at different times."

These are the words of a Columbia University rebel. The point is well taken: Everyone is nineteen. The issue, however, is whether or not it is different to be nineteen in the late 1960s and early 1970s.

What will happen to the college revolutionaries as they leave the university and move out into the world? No one, including myself, would be pretentious enough to try to answer this question with any certainty. There are, however, some apparent trends, and we are already beginning to feel their impact.

In the Army dissent is a major issue, on a scale unprecedented in the history of this nation. Radical newspapers are being published, antiwar coffeehouses are being opened, and military discipline is no longer accepted at its face value. The college graduate in the Army wants to be shown that the exercise of military authority over him is both right and necessary —the same standard he uses for all other authority.

Before the Selective Service boards of our nation, we are hearing an increasing number of students say, "I am a conscientious objector to this particular war. I will not fight an immoral war." And the students are gaining support from the most genuinely establishmentarian circles. At least one Federal district judge has written some sympathetic words in a recent opinion. Moreover, the National Conference of Catholic Bishops has asked that the law of the land be amended to permit conscientious objection to a particular war.

The activities of the college revolutionaries are not related just to the military or to the war they so despise. They are beginning to permeate other areas of our society.

As any Roman Catholic knows, the most powerful moving force for change in the American church comes from the young. It comes from not only the young revolutionary college student, but the young seminarian. Together they have put pressures on parish churches to modernize the liturgy, to make it more meaningful and more personal. Pressures on bishoprics to spend more money on social problems and less on big churches are increasing. Underground Masses are being held all over the country. The search for a more personal, individualistic religious experience is continuing beyond the university.

The law firms of our nation, particularly the large ones, are already feeling the pressure from the new breed of young lawyers. They want deeper involvement in the social problems of the day. Law review graduates will no longer work for law firms which are concerned only with "making money for people who have too much already or increasing the size of corporations which are already too big." They want involvement in the ghetto; involvement in unpopular civil rights causes; involvement across the spectrum of American life; and they want it on the job, not at night after work. They regard it as an essential part of a satisfying career. Like Western European students, they will no longer separate "bread-and-butter" work from "meaningful" work. Ask them why and they say, "Why not? We do not have to." And they are right.

In the law firms, things may become even more difficult. For the May 1969 issue of the *Harvard Law School Record* argues that law students should set standards for law firms. To quote two paragraphs:

> The time is ripe for students to set up standards for the larger firms. For example, we could demand that one afternoon a week be donated to legal aid or other public work. If a student happens to join the self-funding, public-interest law firm program [discussed in detail in the article], we could ask for some type of matching system. Regarding interviewing sessions itself, we could all decide that if a firm engages in 'unfair recruiting practices,' we would boycott it. Furthermore, we could decide that no student will discuss his law school aptitude test scores with an employer because these are inherently even more of an irrational standard than grades; or if pass-fail is approved we could force employers to evaluate written work by refusing to discuss in detail college grades.
>
> Obviously, the specific standards should be for the law student body as a whole to work out. But what is needed now is an agreement among students to follow standards set up and the establishment of a mechanism to propose specific ideas.

The words of the Law School authors speak for themselves. Beyond that, Ralph Nader has shown us what can be done with a small group of public-interest-oriented lawyers and economists. The group is being enlarged substantially.

It is logical that the law firms be one of the initial groups hit, because many lawyers are essentially social scientists and so motivated. It is also logical that the university faculties become increasingly staffed with young New-Left thinkers, since faculties too are at the forefront of social activity.

But where else does the student revolutionary go? What about business? Medicine? Government? Even here we are seeing some of the talents of the young rebels at work. In government, no one can walk through the offices of OEO without noting the relatively large number of middle-level bureaucrats who are quite different from any others in the Federal establishment. They are better motivated, but they are also motivated for revolutionary change.

In Washington, as noted, we have witnessed the formation of the Federal Employees for a Democratic Society. Originally headed by Madeleine Golde, a young employee in the Office of Juvenile Delinquency, this group now claims representatives in most bureaus of the Federal government. To use the words of one of its early founders, it has the capability of "operating as a shadow government." The organization began in the Spring of 1968 as a result of a Vietnam war protest organized by a few young Federal workers. Its membership in the summer of 1969 was about 250, very much alive and growing.

Independent of the Federal Employees for a Democratic Society, a group of employees in the Department of Health, Education and Welfare publishes a monthly newspaper, *The Advocate*. Any issue of *The Advocate* contains attacks on existing government policies, from racism in mental health to the sale of California grapes in the HEW cafeteria, to the personnel policy of HEW and the Civil Service Commission. Perhaps for one of the first times in modern history, this group of employees wrote to the then Cabinet Secretary John Gardner in December 1967 attacking the proposed mandatory work training

88

provision for mothers and the proposed freeze for the number of children on the welfare rolls, and *they refused to carry out the policy of that law if it were passed.*

One can write them off as a few radicals, but not without noting that they now control Local No. 41 of the American Federation of Government Employees (the union with jurisdiction over the Office of the Secretary, the Social and Rehabilitation Service, and most of the Public Health Service); that they forced Secretary Robert Finch to remove California grapes from the HEW cafeteria; and that they sit on task forces developing government programs.

Moreover, they do not consider this more than the most embryonic beginning. Perhaps the point is best made by Mike Tabor, a bushy-haired, heavy-set young man, now working in the Department of Health, Education, and Welfare, who emphasizes that they are not student revolutionaries. In his words, "SDS is a lot different now than it was when I was in college four years ago. The radicals haven't even hit the beach yet."

When I asked Tabor whether he was concerned about radicals' activity in the government, he replied that his main concern was that the public nature of their activity would bring "repressive measures" before such measures were really warranted and before the radicals could get enough basic work done. As Tabor, a 1965 graduate of the University of Maryland's graduate school in education, put it, "There are three options available: co-option, repression, and revolution. There is some movement afoot now to co-opt the blacks and credential the rest of us; that is, take us into the system. We will not go along with this if it means the same dehumanizing experience which has so corrupted our parents. We don't want repression before we have gotten the revolution off the ground."

With the ABM issue we have seen the first involvement of young scientists on a major scale in opposition to government policy they consider wrong. Business and labor have not yet had their share of revolutionaries. However, they will. For SDS is willing even to shave in order to bore the corporate and worker establishments from within. The American Medical Association is finding more and more young interns who will not join.

Quo vadis?

Who knows?

The one thing that is clear is that many of our young will persist, at least through the early years of their working lives, in their attempt to change the society in which we live. They would like to change it for the better. The overwhelming majority will do so peacefully if they get the chance. My main concern is not that the students will rise up and destroy the country, but that, if we fail to give them the opportunity to effect peaceful change, we will turn so many of our most talented young Americans into alienated, unfulfilled adults.

As Harvard Law School graduate Weldon Levine noted at the June 1969 Commencement, "You have convinced us that equality and justice were inviolable concepts, and we have taken you seriously."

There is, after all, more than a little truth in the student charge that if you don't help solve the problem, you become a part of it.

Index

Libertinism, hypocritical, 51
Living conditions, 31
London *Observer*, 50
London School of Economics, 17–20, 22, 45, 58
  mistakes of, 51
Look magazine, 73
Mao Tse-tung, 19, 43–44, 64, 79
Maoists, 23
Marcuse, Herbert, 19, 43–44, 64, 79
Marijuana, 60–61
Marxism, 43–44
Mass media, 53–54
Materialism, 44–45
McCarthy, Senator Eugene, 79
McGovern, Senator George, 60–61
Middle class, 55–56
Middle East, nations of, 16
Military discipline, 86
Military training, 38
  Israeli, 37
Military-industrial complex, 62
Mills, C. Wright, 62
Minority groups, 57–60, 81
Molotov cocktails, 33
Morality, 45, 65, 66–67, 77
Mutuality, 71
Nader, Ralph, 87–88
Nanterre University, 20ff.
National Advisory Commission on Selective Service, 74
National Conference of Catholic Bishops, 86
National Union of Students (England), 20
Nationalism, 38–39, 64
NATO, 28
New Democratic Coalition, 68
New York Times Magazine, 66
Newspapers: influence of, 53
  radical, 86
  underground, 83
Nietzsche, 23
Nihilists, 23
Nixon, Richard M., 74, 77
  and draft system, 61
Nuclear Non-proliferation Treaty, 28
Oberlin College, discipline at, 51
Obsolescence, 83

Office of Economic Opportunity, 78, 88
Office of Juvenile Delinquency, 88
Okinawa reversion, 33, 35, 38
Omega point, 66
Osaka World's Fair, 33, 35
Otepka, Otto, 68
Outer-directed elements, 69–70
Overcrowding, 18–19, 21, 27, 28, 31, 46–48, 49–50, 51, 64, 80, 82–83
Pacifists, 25
Palisades High School, Los Angeles, 83
Parents: hypocrisy of, 67–68
  student reaction to, 67
Parent-Teacher Associations, 83
Patriotism, 64
Peace Corps, 51, 78
Permissiveness, 50
Philosophy, adult, 67
Poirier, Richard, 67
Police: brutality, 51
  Japanese, 32
  support, 29
Policy, university, 61–62, 71–79
  administrative, 24
  student participation in, 18–19, 28, 31, 59
Political doctrines, 65
Political parties, 50–51, 64, 79–80
Politicians: hypocrisy of, 68
  opinions of, 62–63
  and university support, 28, 29
Politics: German, 25–26
  hypocrisy of, 44–45
  ideologies of, 62
  and student unrest, 50–51
Pollution, 46–47
Pope Paul VI, 16, 47
Population explosion, 72
Post-industrial nations, 16, 17–29, 30–35, 40–56
  (*see also* England; France; Germany; Italy; Japan; United States; West Berlin; Western Germany)
Powell, Enoch, 46
Power-élite, 62
Pre-industrial nations, 36–39
  students in, 54–55